TAKING CARE OF YOUR

GERBILS

Joyce Pope

Series consultant: Michael Findlay

Photographs by: Sally Anne Thompson
and R T Willbie/Animal Photography

Franklin Watts
London   New York   Toronto   Sydney

The author
Joyce Pope is Enquiries Officer of the Zoology
Department at the British Museum of Natural History
and also gives regular public lectures to children and
adults on a wide range of subjects.

   She is involved with conservation groups and has
written many books on a variety of topics including
European animals, pets and town animals. She is an
enthusiastic pet owner herself and currently keeps
small mammals, two dogs, a cat and a horse.

The consultant
Michael Findlay is a qualified veterinary surgeon whose
involvement has been mainly with pet animals. He is
now an advisor to a pharmaceutical company. He is
involved with Crufts Dog Show each year and is a
member of the Kennel Club. He is president of several
Cat Clubs and is Chairman of the Feline Advisory
Bureau. He currently has three Siamese cats and two
Labrador dogs.

© 1987 Franklin Watts

First published in Great
Britain in 1987 by
Franklin Watts
12a Golden Square
London W1

First published in the
United States of America
by
Franklin Watts Inc.
387 Park Avenue South
New York
N.Y. 10016

Printed in Belgium

UK edition:
ISBN 0 86313 414 9
US edition:
ISBN 0–531–10190–8
Library of Congress
Catalog Card Number:
85–52086

Designed by
Ben White

Illustrated by
Hayward Art Group

Acknowledgments
The photographers and publishers would like to thank
Mr Jim Rowe, Lynton Pet Shop, Gloucester; Mr Neil
Wallace and the families and their gerbils who
participated in the photography for this book.

TAKING CARE OF YOUR

GERBILS

Contents

Introducing pets

People like to keep pets. They add interest to our lives and they are often good company, especially for anybody who is alone or sick. By caring for them and watching them we can find out how other creatures use the world that we think of as ours.

▽ Until about twenty years ago nobody thought of keeping gerbils as pets. Now they are among the most popular of all small animals kept as household pets.

Petkeepers' code

1 A pet is not a toy, but a living creature which has its own feelings and needs.

2 A pet relies on you to give it food and water every day.

3 A pet must have its own living and sleeping place which must be kept clean.

4 A pet relies on you to care for it if it is ill.

5 You are responsible for your pet and what it does.

▽ Gerbils are easy to tame and rarely bite. They need plenty of exercise. When they are tame enough they can get exercise by exploring and playing outside their cage.

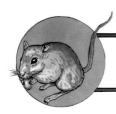

What is a gerbil?

Gerbils are small gnawing animals in the rodent family. Many kinds of gerbils live wild in dry or desert areas of Asia and Africa. Several different types have been captured and kept as pets, but the Mongolian Gerbil is the most common type seen in pet shops. This animal comes from the arid lands between northern China and the Soviet Union.

▽ Mongolian Gerbils make good pets for although they are active and agile animals they are friendly and easy to tame. Males, which weigh about 4½oz (130g) are larger than females, which weigh about 2½oz (70g).

◁ When feeding, gerbils often sit up on their hind legs and hold seeds or other food in their forepaws, which they use like hands.

△ This is an argenti gerbil – one of the few varieties that you might find in a pet shop. They have red eyes and soft, golden-colored coats with no long outer hairs.

Mongolian Gerbils are sandy brown in color. They have long tails, long hind legs and very short front legs. When moving slowly, they walk on all four feet, but if they are frightened in an open space, they leap away on their hind legs like tiny kangaroos.

In the wild, Mongolian Gerbils always live in groups. They dig deep burrows which protect them from hot and cold weather. Like all rodents, gerbils have a pair of chisel-like incisor, or gnawing, teeth in the front of the mouth. These grow throughout the animal's life and must be kept worn down by nibbling on hard substances.

Mongolian Gerbils make very good
pets. They are small and take up
little space. They are quite cheap to
buy and do not cost a lot to feed.
Unlike hamsters, which sleep during
most of the day and become active at
night, Mongolian Gerbils sleep for
short periods and are then active
throughout the day and night.

They are desert animals that are
able to conserve water in their
bodies and because of this they do
not smell as much as most other
small animals.

△ Mother gerbils usually
produce families of four
babies. This black variety
has been bred in the last
few years, but is not
common.

◁ Some varieties of gerbils have a mixture of colors, like this black and white one.

Other advantages of having gerbils as pets is that although they are active and inquisitive they are very friendly and they hardly ever bite. Also, they are quiet, so they will not disturb your neighbors.

Mongolian Gerbils were first taken from their homelands to Japan in 1945. In 1964 some were sent to America and in the same year some arrived in Europe. At first they were used as laboratory animals but soon people realized that they made good pets.

Because gerbils have been kept as pets for such a short time, very few varieties of color or fur type have yet developed.

△ This albino gerbil has completely white fur and bright pink eyes. In the wild its noticeable appearance would be a danger to it, but as a pet, it is protected by its owner.

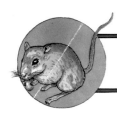

Preparing for a gerbil

Before you get a gerbil you must be sure that you have the time and the money to care for your pet. Also you must have your parents' permission, as they will probably have to help you to look after it from time to time.

You must also find a suitable place to keep the animal. It should not be in a drafty spot, nor in direct sunlight, though it must not be in a dark corner either.

△ Your gerbil's cage should have a thick layer of peat or wood shavings (but never sawdust) on the floor. For their sleeping quarters you can buy a special bedding material from your pet shop or you can use hay.

◁ Some cages have several "floors" so that gerbils can get exercise running up and down.

The most important thing to prepare for your pet is the cage. Gerbils are sometimes housed in hamster cages, but these are not really suitable, as gerbils are burrowers. They will constantly kick out pieces of bedding as they reorganize their living place. It is better to buy or build a cage made of metal or hard plastic. It should be at least 24in (60cm) long, 12in (30cm) high and 10in (25cm) wide.

You will also need a supply of floor covering for the cage – garden peat is quite good – and hay for bedding. You'll need to buy food and water containers and a week's supply of food in advance.

▽ A home-made cage for gerbils can be designed to fit a particular place, so you can make the best of the space available for your pets.

◁ You will probably need the help of a grown-up if you decide to make a cage. It has to be strong enough to prevent your gerbils from escaping. Here is an old aquarium being converted into a gerbilarium.

11

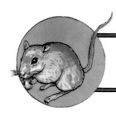

Better homes for gerbils

Gerbils are burrowing animals. They are best kept in a place with deep bedding in which they can dig as much as they please without making a mess. You could get stacking cages. You will need at least three levels to keep two gerbils properly. Or you could get a metal cage.

Better still is to house your gerbils in a gerbilarium. Make this in a glass or plastic tank about 24in (60cm) long, 16in (40cm) wide and 12in (30cm) high. An old aquarium is ideal for this.

◁ Although these cages are well ventilated, they must not be put in direct sunlight, as they could overheat very easily. Never put the cage where it will be exposed to drafts.

Fill your gerbilarium to a depth of at least 4in (10cm) with a mixture of moss peat, sterilized compost, chopped straw and a little charcoal. Make it as firm as you can.

Put a few pieces of clean branches and other toys on the surface. Add some hay and a heavy food bowl. The water bottle can be fixed to the top or the side of the tank.

The gerbils will burrow into the soil and make tunnels and nests as though they were in the wild.

▽ A properly made gerbilarium is very heavy, so it must have a strong support. Once it has been set up, a gerbilarium needs little attention other than checking the water and putting in fresh food. It only needs to be cleaned out completely about every 2 or 3 months.

△ Gerbils don't seem to notice that you can watch them through the glass sides of the gerbilarium. They are too busy digging tunnels!

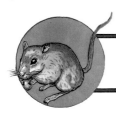

Choosing gerbils

A gerbil forced to live on its own will almost certainly be very unhappy, so be prepared to get two. You may have a friend who has some baby gerbils who need homes, but you will get a better choice in a pet shop.

   You should buy gerbils when they are about 5 or 6 weeks old. Get two of the same sex. Two females should live together peaceably.

▽ It is often difficult to tell the sex of young gerbils but the breeder or pet shop owner will be able to help you. It is best to get two females from the same litter as these will settle down well together.

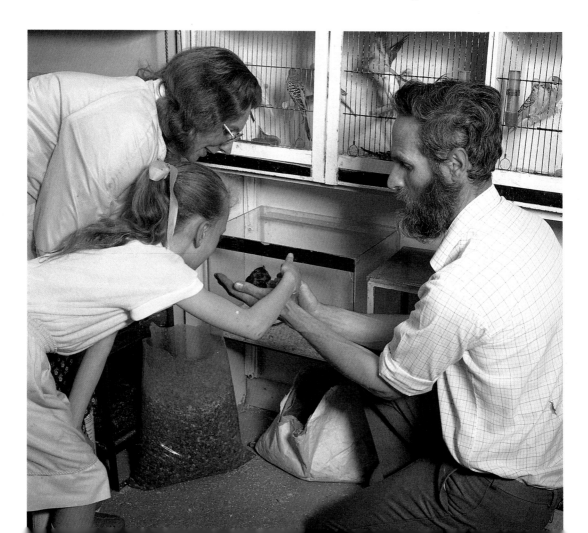

Choose gerbils which are alert, active and curious about everything. Do not get any that seem to be timid, for these may be difficult to tame and may be ill.

A healthy gerbil should have a sleek coat, with no sign of baldness or of sores. Its eyes should be bright and not watering. Its nose should be clean and have no sign of any discharge. Its teeth should not show when the animal closes its mouth.

Look at the fur under the animal's tail – it should be quite clean. If it is stained with droppings, the gerbil probably has an upset stomach which may be difficult to cure.

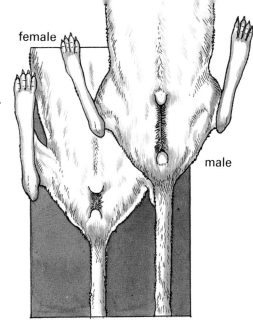

△ To tell which sex your gerbil is look at the underside of the animal. The male is shown above on the right; the female is shown on the left.

◁ A healthy gerbil should be active and bright-eyed.

Your gerbils at home

◁ Your gerbils will probably begin to make themselves at home by rearranging their bedding or digging tunnels in the soil of their gerbilarium.

You should carry your gerbils home as quickly but as gently as possible. As soon as you arrive home, put them into the gerbilarium or cage that you have prepared.

Remember that they may be very young and leaving the rest of their family is a big change for them. Although you will probably want to tame them right away, you should leave them to explore and settle down in their new home for a while.

Baby gerbils are the easiest small animals to tame because they are so curious. Hold out a tidbit, such as a sunflower seed, on your hand. The gerbils will come to see what it is and take it from you. It may take them several days to lose their shyness but then you can try to stroke one while it is feeding.

Soon your gerbil will be ready to come right on to your hand. Cup your other hand around it but be careful not to frighten it or it may jump off and hurt itself.

▽ Once they've settled in, one way of picking up a gerbil is to hold it by the base of the tail (never the tip which is very fragile) and to put it on your hand. Keep hold of the base of the tail, until you are sure it is quite tame.

Gerbils may collapse if they are frightened by being handled. If this happens put the animal back into its cage quickly and gently.

◁ Let your gerbils settle into their surroundings before trying to tame them.

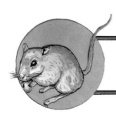

Feeding your gerbils

Gerbils are plant-eating animals, needing between $\frac{1}{3}$oz to $\frac{2}{3}$oz (10 and 20gm) of food a day. If you do not have scales to weigh this amount, about a tablespoonful each should be enough.

If it is all eaten quickly, give them a little more, but you will soon find the right quantity for your pets.

Commercially available gerbil pellets will provide your gerbil with a balanced diet. This can be supplemented with small amounts of fruits, vegetables and shelled nuts.

△ Your pets must always have clean water. It is best to supply this in a bottle, where it cannot get fouled or dirty. Although gerbils do not take a lot of water, they quickly learn to use the bottle and drink about a teaspoonful of water a day.

◁ It is probably easiest for you to feed your gerbils at whatever time you check and clean their cage, for they need to be fed only once a day. They are unlikely to overeat, except when they are given a lot of sunflower seeds, which are addictive to gerbils and therefore not recommended.

As a special treat gerbils may also be given raisins, small pieces of cheese and occasionally some bird seed. It is particularly useful to offer these to your pets when you are trying to tame them, for they will learn to associate you with things that they like to eat.

△ If the water bottle is not in an upright position, you must make sure that it is more than half full or no water will come out.

As well as dry food, gerbils should have some fresh vegetables and fruit each day. This won't make them expensive pets to keep, as the amounts that they eat are quite small.

Leave a bit more than usual round the core of an apple, or take a slice from the carrots being prepared for your meal. You will then have enough fresh food for your two gerbils for one day.

They are fond of melon seeds and will chew the last scrap of flesh from the rind of a melon. In fact, you can give them a little of almost any raw fruit or vegetable that you eat.

△ Some ideal fresh food for gerbils.

▽ Be sure to remove any uneaten scraps of fresh food from your gerbils' cage each day. If you do not, the scraps will go bad very quickly and may give your pets serious digestive troubles.

You can collect wild plants for your gerbils. These can include grasses, which they may chop up and add to their bedding; dandelions, both flowers and leaves; the tips of bramble shoots and chickweed.

Do not give them buttercups, which are poisonous. Be very careful when you gather any wild plants. Pick them away from a main road, as the plants will be polluted by the fumes from the traffic. Also be sure that anything you take has not been sprayed with a herbicide or insecticide, or been fouled by animals.

△ Gerbils like a little fresh fruit and vegetable every day for variety.

▽ You should always wash and dry any wild plants before giving them to your gerbils.

Gerbil toys

You can make the lives of your gerbils more interesting by giving them toys. These will help them to be active and keep healthy. One of the best toys is an exercise wheel. Your pet shop will have several kinds. You should get one with a solid back and wheel. A gerbil could break its tail or its leg in one of the slatted wheels that are sometimes sold.

▽ One of the best toys for gerbils is the tube from the middle of a roll of kitchen paper or foil. The gerbils will enjoy running through the tunnel of cardboard but they will soon tear it into small pieces which they will add to their bedding.

Gerbil toys need not cost a lot. But gerbils explore their toys by chewing at them and will quickly destroy anything that is not very tough. You should not give your pets objects that could be harmful, that are brittle or that might be gnawed to make a sharp edge.

A clay flower pot or a herb pot with holes through which gerbils can squeeze makes a good toy. You can add a piece of branch, on which gerbils can climb and nibble at to keep their teeth short.

△ Gerbils enjoy gnawing on a small piece of hard wood and shredding kitchen towels and plain paper. You should not give them newspaper, as the printing ink is poisonous to them. Also, you should never give your pets baby toys, as the wool from which these toys are often made can block the gerbils' intestines.

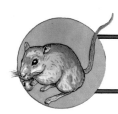

Gerbil hygiene

A healthy gerbil always looks clean and shiny, yet you will find that your pets, unlike most other small animals, do not spend a great deal of their time grooming themselves.

The reason for this is that as they burrow through the deep covering of litter on the floor of their cage, their fur is "combed" by the dry walls of their tunnels. This removes any scraps of dirt or scurf or grease from their coats.

△ Gerbils clean themselves naturally by rolling in peat. Some gerbils may deposit their droppings in one corner of their cage. If so, you can scrape these out every few days without disturbing the animals. Check that the water bottle does not leak or get plugged up with bedding.

Gerbils smell very little to our noses. This does not mean that you do not have to attend to the gerbils' cage, but you need only clean it out completely every two or three weeks. You should then remove the gerbils to a safe place while you wash the cage out with warm water and disinfectant. After rinsing the cage thoroughly, make sure it is quite dry before putting in new floor covering and bedding.

If you have a gerbilarium, it can be left for a longer time without being cleaned out. Two to three months should be often enough. You will probably need the help of an adult.

△ When you wash out the gerbils' cage make sure the gerbils are put in a safe place where you can keep an eye of them. After you have been handling or playing with your pets, you should always wash your hands.

Gerbil health

If you get healthy young gerbils and keep them sensibly, they should not suffer from illness. But if a gerbil is less active than usual, or its coat is dull or its eyes and nose are runny, take it to your veterinarian. Many gerbil illnesses can be fatal if they are not treated quickly.

▽ Gerbils have scent glands which look like small bald patches on their undersides. Sometimes these become infected. If so, it is wisest to take the animal to the vet for treatment.

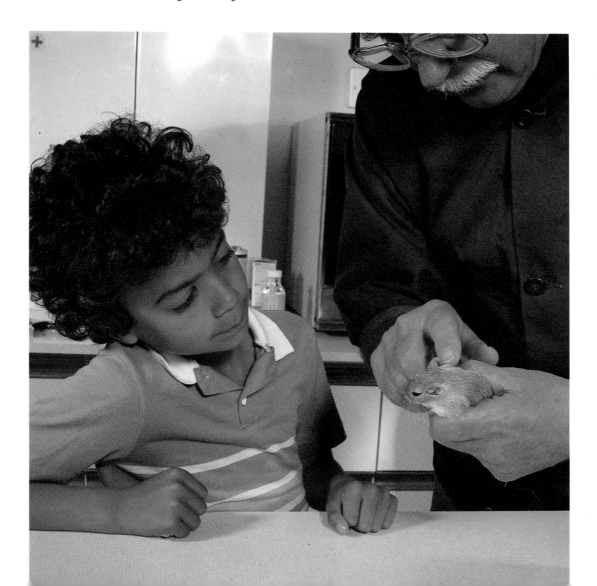

Sometimes gerbils are injured through fighting. If one of your pets is badly bitten you should take it to the veterinarian. You can bathe a small cut with weak disinfectant and it should heal easily.

If you handle a gerbil too much or too roughly it may get upset. You should put the animal back into its cage and remember to treat it much more gently in future.

Gerbils should be kept out of drafts or they may catch colds. They prefer a temperature of about 70°F (21°C). If gerbils get too hot they may suffer from heat stroke. If so, they should be put in a cool, dark place and given plenty of water.

△ If gerbils do not have enough hard things to chew, their incisor teeth may become overgrown. If this happens, a vet can clip the teeth to the right length.

▷ Diseases can be passed from wild mice to gerbils, so always keep your pets' food and bedding in a place where it cannot be contaminated. Remember that good hygiene will help to keep your gerbils healthy.

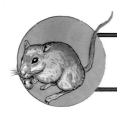

Finding out more

Gerbils become tame so easily that you can soon allow them out of their cage. Make quite sure there is no cat or dog around which might harm them.

Gerbils love to explore in your pockets or on the table. Watch how they find out about anything new. Do they sniff it or touch it with their whiskers or their paws first?

△ Time how long it takes your gerbils to do a particular thing. When you write it in your gerbil diary, put the date and the time of day. You may find that they do things differently as they get older, or at different times of the day or year.

28

You can find out a great deal about your gerbils by keeping a gerbil diary, in which you write down the things that they do. It is important to note even ordinary things like sleeping and eating.

Find out whether they sleep curled up or stretched out. Do they hold their food in their front paws? How do they deal with a big piece of food, like a large carrot or a whole apple? Do they carry favorite food like sunflower seeds away to hide in a private place? How long does it take them to begin to play with a new toy?

▽ It is always interesting to see the reaction of a gerbil to a new sort of food or a new toy.

△ Try to discover if your gerbils are all active. If not, what are the differences between them? Your findings could be part of your gerbil project.

Checklist

 Before you get your gerbils:

1 Be sure that you have your parents' permission.
2 Be sure that you have a proper place to keep them and a secure cage which is big enough.
3 Be sure that you have time to look after them.
4 Get at least a week's supply of dry food.

 Daily check:

1 Give your pets their dry food.
2 Remove any uneaten bits of fruit or vegetable and replace with fresh green food or fruit.
3 Check the water bottle and refill.
4 Check that your gerbils have plenty of bedding.

 Weekly check:

1 Wash out the food bowls and water bottle carefully.
2 Make sure that your pets still have some hard wood to gnaw. Replace it if necessary.
3 Make sure that you have enough dry food to last through the coming week.
4 Check that your pets' teeth and claws are not overgrown and that their coats are healthy and shiny.

 Biweekly check:

1 Put the gerbils in a safe place and clean the cage with mild disinfectant. Rinse and dry it thoroughly.
2 Put in new bedding, but keep a little from the previous bedding.
3 Wash and dry all toys.

Questions and answers

Q Is it better to have one gerbil or two?

A Gerbils like company, so it is far better to keep two. It is better to get two females, which will live together without fighting. If you get a male and a female they will breed. You would then have the problem of disposing of baby gerbils.

Q How long do gerbils live?

A Well-looked-after gerbils should live for about 3 years and they may survive for up to 5 years.

Q How many kinds of tame gerbils are there?

A About six different kinds of gerbils are sometimes kept as pets.

Q What is the scientific name of the kind of gerbil usually kept as a pet?

A *Meriones unguiculatus*, the Mongolian Gerbil is the kind most usually kept as a pet.

Q What is the best way to make gerbils tame?

A Let them settle into their new home, then try to tempt them to come to you for a tidbit. They love raisins or little pieces of cheese. They will soon learn to associate you with something specially nice and will come to you trustingly. Do not give them too much of these foods, as this could harm them.

Index